KU-061-138

Alice Walker won the Pulitzer Prize and the National Book Award for her novel *The Color Purple*. Her other bestselling novels include *By the Light of My Father's Smile*, *Possessing the Secret of Joy* and *The Temple of My Familiar*. She is also the author of several collections of short stories, essays and poetry, as well as children's books. Her work has been translated into more than two dozen languages, and her books have sold over 15 million copies. Born in Eatonton, Georgia, Alice Walker now shares her time between Mexico, Hawaii and northern California.

Visit Alice Walker's official website at:
alicewalkersgarden.com

By the same author

Fiction
The Color Purple
The Third Life of Grange Copeland
Meridian
Possessing the Secret of Joy
You Can't Keep a Good Woman Down
In Love and Trouble
The Temple of My Familiar
The Complete Stories
By the Light of My Father's Smile
The Way Forward Is with a Broken Heart
Now Is the Time to Open Your Heart

Poetry
Horses Make a Landscape Look More Beautiful
Once
Good Night, Willie Lee, I'll See You in the Morning
Revolutionary Petunias and Other Poems
Her Blue Body Everything We Know
A Poem Travelled Down My Arm
Absolute Trust in the Goodness of the Earth
Alice Walker: Collected Poems

Non-Fiction
In Search of Our Mothers' Gardens
Living by the Word
Anything We Love Can Be Saved
Sent by Earth: A Message from the Grandmother Spirit
Warrior Marks (with Pratibha Parmer)
The Same River Twice: Honoring the Difficult
The Chicken Chronicles

TAKING THE ARROW OUT OF THE HEART

Poems

ALICE WALKER

WEIDENFELD & NICOLSON

First published in Great Britain in 2018
by Weidenfeld & Nicolson
an imprint of The Orion Publishing Group Ltd
Carmelite House, 50 Victoria Embankment
London EC4Y 0DZ

An Hachette UK Company

1 3 5 7 9 10 8 6 4 2

Copyright © Alice Walker 2018

The moral right of Alice Walker to be identified as
the author of this work has been asserted in accordance
with the Copyright, Designs and Patents Act of 1988.

All rights reserved. No part of this publication may be
reproduced, stored in a retrieval system, or transmitted in any form
or by any means, electronic, mechanical,photocopying, recording, or
otherwise, without the prior permission of both the copyright
owner and the above publisher of this book.

All the characters in this book are fictitious, and any resemblance
to actual persons, living or dead, is purely coincidental.

A CIP catalogue record for this book is
available from the British Library.

ISBN (Mass Market Paperback) 978 1 4746 0726 1
ISBN (eBook) 978 1 4746 0727 8

Text designed by Kyoko Watanabe

Printed and bound in Great Britain by Clays Ltd, Elcograf S.p.A.

www.orionbooks.co.uk

Remembering Coretta Scott King
generous and kind
brightly smiling;
happy.
Before the arrow struck.

And with respect, to David Icke
the "mad" one;
connecting dots, finding arrows,
removing them too
when people help.

And for all of us who have ever fallen:
who have removed the arrow
sometimes many times
and stood up
again.

If we want a better world,
we have to make it ourselves.
—A. W.

CONTENTS

Introduction

No one escapes a time in life when the arrow of sorrow, of anger, of despair pierces the heart. For many of us, there is the inevitable need to circle the wound. It is often such a surprise to find it there, in us, when we had assumed arrows so painful only landed in the hearts of other people. Some of us spend decades screaming at the archer. Or at least for longer periods than are good for us. How to take the arrow out of the heart? How to learn to relieve our own pain? That is the question. Like many such questions it is delved into by Buddhism, but also by anyone who has lived long enough to see—by trial and error, for the most part—that the futility we begin to feel, as we attempt to bring down the archer, leaves our wounded heart untended, and the medicine of Life that abounds wherever we are is left unapplied.

Taking the Arrow Out of the Heart was not the original title of this new book, poems written mainly in 2015–2016. It was a time of great sadness and feelings of loss and despair. Worse to face, as now, are the brutal murders of children, the deliberate starving and abusing of them. The callous trampling on their rights as human beings, however small, and the brutal indifference (as they must experience it) of the grown-up world. Entwined with this is the abuse of the planet, the literal draining of her blood, the carving up for profit of her very flesh and bone.

And yet, there are those of us humans who have stood up, wherever we could stand up, in defense of children, animals, the earth, and we have had ancestors before us who have done the same. Which is how we learned. One such ancestor was Muhammad Ali. That fierce, indignant poet of words and fists. Though he was not alone. This book originally carried a title celebrating his courageous walk through a challenging life, and a battered but triumphant exit from it: *The Long Road Home.*

I still love this idea—that to remain on that road "home" to the truest self we can muster is a knockout in the ring of life. And to achieve, even to approach, or get on that road home! Maybe to actually get your whole self there . . . this would be bliss beyond imagining. For then we would surely join the Immortals: those who laid out the path as best they could for us, by their example. Which, in so many instances, was all they had. Imagine. Owning only the example of one's behavior. When applied to our people and to so many peoples we are now discovering, we begin to see our inherited riches. Our inherited wealth. It is the road itself.

But life will change course. And so I was invited to give a talk at a university and the instruction that rose again and again in me from the Source that always knows how plagued with doubt and confusion and guilt humans are, was "talk to them about how that arrow many feel in their hearts is not theirs alone. Remind them it is worthwhile to train to learn how to remove it."

I understood this. Because, indeed, the long road home has many archers waiting in ambush. This reality is part of what keeps the drug industry flourishing. Here, as a poet, I intervene.

TAKING THE
ARROW OUT OF
THE HEART

The Long Road Home

for Muhammad Ali

I am beginning to comprehend
the mystery
of the gift of suffering.
It is true as some
have said
that it is a crucible
in which the gold of one's spirit
is rendered,
and shines.

Ali,
you represent all of us
who stand the test of suffering
most often alone
because who can understand
who or what
has brought us to our feet?

Their knees worn out
ancestors stood us up
from the awkward position
they had to honor
on the floor beneath
the floor.

I have been weeping
all day
thinking of this.
The cloud of witness
the endless teaching
the long road home.

Breathing

Breathing in
I thank Thich Nhat Hanh.
Breathing out
I thank him more.

Here It Is!

for Jesse Williams

Here it is
the beauty that scares you
—so you believe—
to death.
For he is certainly gorgeous
and he is certainly where whiteness
to your disbelief
has not wandered off
to die.
No. It is there, tawny skin, gray eyes,
a Malcolm-esque jaw. His loyal parents
may Goddess bless them
sitting proud and happy and no doubt
amazed
at what they have done.
For he is black too. And obviously
with a soul
made of everything.
Try to think bigger than you ever have
or had courage enough to do:
that blackness is not where whiteness
wanders off to die: but that it is
like the dark matter
between stars and galaxies in
the Universe
that ultimately
holds it all
together.

The New Dark Ages
for Martin

As we slip into the new Dark Ages
you become more dear to me.
Your face, your smile
that carefully trimmed
never to turn gray hair.

We may not emerge from this darkness
in my lifetime.

And yet, I think of you
so often smiling,
or laughing outright;
your sturdy frame gallant
and ready for the fight.

Though it is true
you left home
like the Buddha
to find a way for all of us,
leaving your wife and children
to suffer
a most peculiar loneliness;
and yes,
the children, some of them
would be lost.

Still,
We miss you. Dreadfully.
As we miss
so many others
who left us with this one
desire:
that no matter how deep the fall
into obscurity and obscenity this new age
portends
Life might permit us

to remain standing
if only on the inside;

smiling and laughing
with you

among the solemn army
who went out
into the darkness
all those years ago,
always singing,
to examine the path

and *be* the light.

Loving Oakland

If gentrifiers do not despoil it
which means getting rid of poor
and black and people of color
people
Oakland can be what it has been
for a long time: an urban Paradise.

It is a place where
the young blonde woman
crossing the street in front of your car
would look like a threat
to the neighborhood
except she's frowning
over some deep issue in her inner life
and wearing outrageous vivid blue shoes.

It is a place where
as you sit on the grass by the lake
a tall black man of a certain age
strolls by
blowing his saxophone.
You smile and bow,
he bows back,
with his horn. His day is mellow.
He's in the sun.
He has given mellowness
and sun, free of charge,
to you.

Here
I have found a previously
unexplored
love of sports.
At least I love the Warriors.
Something about basketball
is so graceful, the players so serious,
skilled, nonviolent

and intense; I sit grunting and groaning
like everyone around me; we are
for a short time, family, and these are our brothers
engaged in peaceful war.
I love it that the state house
wears blue and yellow
in long emphatic lights
the whole season
the team is playing
and that our waitress
wears blue and gold earrings
and shakes her curly dark hair
to make sure
we notice them.

Loving Oaklandia:
Frida and Diego would have.
Frida never liked Chicago and actually suffered
in New York City. In Oakland she could spread her
lovely dresses around her on the grass in that new place
designed for sitting and lying
at the far end of the lake.
Diego would appreciate the murals
that are sometimes several stories
high. He'd want to paint his own.
Of course he would!

Whoever said "there is no there there," and I think we are
wrong to think Gertrude Stein
meant this and wasn't joking
(though who knows what Oakland was in her time; or what
she was in Oakland's time)
when she is alleged to have said this.

Because, and thanks, many claim, to Jerry Brown's
foresight about cleaning up the lake,
there is plenty of "there" in Oakland.

―――

It is not just its streets, its good places to eat and play
with one's children and families,
not just the lake, which people love
with so much devotion (though they might never
call it that); it is that smile that hits you in the heart
every time it happens
when a total stranger greets you on the path;
the way the hefty sistahs are admired
by all who see them as they hustle by, arms swinging,
knowingly improving the view
by making it real
and completely enjoying
their daily exercise; it is the sense
that something that was alive
for a very long time
is still alive. Not yet beaten into
submission
or oblivion
by those who kill everything
they touch
with money.

Is Celie Actually Ugly?

for Cynthia Erivo

Is Celie actually ugly?
Asks the charismatic star playing her
on Broadway.
How many times over the years
I have explained
this.
Celie and her "prettier" sister Nettie
are practically identical.
They might be twins.
But Life has forced on Celie
all the hardships
Nettie mostly avoids: a hazy anxiety surrounding
the lynching of her father when she was very small,
repeated rape,
a mother's withheld love
that morphed into
distrust and disdain,
her children, for all she knows,
murdered by
the rapist psychopath who claims
to be her father.
Endless labor that would
demean and soon obliterate
the observable loveliness
of the most queenly slave.
I wanted us to think about
how superficial is our understanding
of beauty; but, also, how beauty
is destroyed.
And how, to bear our own disgrace
these hundreds of years
we've taught ourselves
to laugh at anyone
as abused and diminished
as we feel.
It is Celie's designation

as "nigger of the universe"
by heartless sufferers around her
that makes her "ugly" to them;
they who cannot see, until Love of Herself
lights the dreariness of Celie's existence,
that
the beauty of her
resilient spirit
has become one with the compassionate
loveliness
of
her face.

The World Is Standing Up for Palestine

The world is standing up
for Palestine;
I realized this today
when I discovered a book group
where people
from my own
hoodwinked
country
have
decided to offer
a "humorous" book
to its readers
about Palestine.
Honestly, by now
it is an almost impossible
human endeavor
to think "humorously"
about Palestine.
There is something
about the deliberate targeting
of children's eyes
young people's bright hopes
the beating
and killing of women
the indiscriminate battering down
and slaughter
of old and young men,
house demolitions
and the seemingly
unending bombing of hospitals
and schools
that keeps us from
actually
laughing.

Yet, I happen to know
this book they are offering

and it is very funny.*
I met the woman who wrote
it and listened while
she read from it
with zest
to a packed house
in Ramallah.
She cracked us up.

And that is the spirit
our own country people
are awakening to,
standing up for,
recognizing at last:
for it is a grace
some lucky ones of us
have read about
and even witnessed
or even practiced
in our own diseased
and ripped moral landscape
of no repair.

* Sharon and My Mother-in-Law, *the acclaimed memoir by Palestinian author and architect Suad Amiry*

Wherever You Are Grieving

It does not matter to me:
wherever you are grieving
whether Paris, Damascus, Jerusalem, Bamako,
Mexico or Beirut or New York City
my heart, too, is bruised
and dragging.
There used to be such a thing
as melodrama
when feelings could be
made up,
but now there is bare pain
and sorrow,
a sense of endlessly missed
opportunities
to smile and embrace
"The other."
We mourn the loss
of goodness
that was so divinely
ordinary:
babyhood
youth
the blessings of maturity
and of old age.
All sacrificed now
almost predictably
to the same Greed
our histories
—every one of them—
could have warned us against
if only we knew them.

To Have Once

For years I meditated
peacefully
in this small ruined retreat.
It was whole until the hurricane.
All around it now are fallen trees,
broken limbs,
broken windows
broken doors.

Many roofs in the neighborhood
and in the *pueblo,* both palapa
and tile, are gone.
Nothing,
it appears,
has remained
unscathed.

Everything is trashed.

There is a feeling of unreality,
of sadness that so much beauty
and peace of solitude
has been destroyed,
but overwhelmingly there is
gratitude.

Our beautiful friends and their beautiful children
are alive.

No one was injured, and no one died
from the tempestuous winds
and drowning rain of Hurricane Patricia,
who charted her course
right to the places
most out of the way
—or so we thought—
of unwelcome visitors.

Impermanence. So the Buddha taught.
And, to have once is to have
forever:
so certain of the Aboriginal peoples
believe.

They Will Always Be More Beautiful Than You

I

They will always be
more beautiful
than you
the people you are killing.
You think it is hatred
that you feel
but it is really envy.
You imagine if you destroy them

we will forget

how tall they stood

how level
their gaze
how straight their backs.
How even the littlest ones
stood their little ground.

Meanwhile
you stand
hunched as a cobbler
in your absurd
killer's gear
yelling
like a crazy person,
your face contorted
dripping sweat
from what would be
with or without
your lethal weapons
a bullying brow
and feral chin.

——

Killing everyone
but especially children,
for sport.

Looking cool
in your own mind;
as you crunch bones
beneath your boot
that are still
forming.

Conquering.

II

Don't forget the entertainment value

of your daily work
for the folks back home.
Who witness from the hillsides
in their lounge chairs.

What beautiful fun!

We are not like
those people being broken
over there
they tell each other. And for this moment
they are right.
They are not.

But what does this mean
for broken humanity?

Selfie this.

Imagine

We can only imagine
what these two—
Francis and Fidel—
really had to say
to each other.
The Pope wondering
who really is the Holy Father here,
since everything he's
preaching as holy
Fidel has already
fulfilled.
Fidel
seeing humor
in the Argentine's unmistakable
Italian roots
and thinking pointedly
but not saying
politely,
like the good Jesuit
and Revolutionary he is:
My people have suffered
long enough:
Don't mess this up.
God, it took you forever
to get to be Pope,
I imagine him saying
aloud.
You know it did!
Francis might reply.
And you know
exactly why:
that place I work at is a den
of murderers and thieves.
And if their stuff hadn't
hit the fan:
evidence of
priests impregnating

captive Indigenous teens
in the past
and buggering white altar boys
in the present;
and folks starting to notice
the amount of stolen gold
and property
we have (enough to house, feed and clothe
pretty much every poor person on the planet)
they would never
have put me out here.
Climate Change
or no Climate Change.
I know, says Fidel.
They're clever that way.
I used to wonder how you
stood it: sitting at the back
all those years
while they ruled
the world from every
parliament and throne.
Horrifically, too,
we can add.
And what about that apology business
that's always trotted out?
They're guilty of the torture and murder
of Earth and Her Peoples all over the place.
De Las Casas, for one, has told us
some of the worst of it.
And now they want to get away
with an *apology*!
Some don't even want to do that, says Francis.
If the violated and exploited
took back their stolen lands and goods
from your fellow churchmen
and brutally drove them out of house
and home, after killing their parents
and enslaving their children,
would *they* be satisfied with an apology?

Oh, it's been a challenge, all right.
I can testify to that, says Francis,
waving aside a camera.
And a personal one, for me:
it's no fun
especially as you age,
to recognize your role
as a Conquistador
of Spirit.
A conqueror
of the people's very spirits and souls!
The very definition of "devil"
I sometimes think.
When folks bow to me
I want to shout at them: bowing
to your masters
is what you were forced to do in the first place:
Straighten up!
And how bizarre that they want me to kiss their babies!

That *is* chilling, says Fidel. It isn't as if our people
are ignorant of witch burnings
and the Inquisition. Even if they haven't studied
Reservations in El Norte and
Indian boarding schools.
But cheer up. Who could have imagined
what the world is really like
when we were children?
We're old now, but in spite of all we learned,
so much of it dreadful and scary, even
petrifying,
we gave Life
our best shot.
Perfection will have
to wait for the next incarnation.
And I mean of the world, not just us.

Refugees

They would not be running to us
if we were not chasing them
with the guns and bombs and rockets we sold
to crazy people:
out of their houses
out of their schools
out of their mosques,
churches,
synagogues
away from their favorite
prayer trees.
You are guilty America
of arming the world:
if you could,
and to make money
you'd arm the Universe.
Remember
Ronald Reagan
talking about
Star Wars
when he could barely
walk
let alone
handle a laser?
That's how deep it is
our country's need to control
the earth
that it never seems to care about
otherwise.
But it is not our country
that is at fault
it is the entities
who have taken it over.
Who might not even be
from here,
which is my own belief.
But from some distant star

they camouflaged as "heaven"
to make us think they were special;
angels even. And not rapists of planets
through the terror
and manipulation
of war.

The World Rising

The world rising
can put an end
to anything:
the murder of children
whales
elephants
forests
oceans.
Get up. Roll over
on that part
of you
that will not
welcome
recognize
encourage
or even see
our rise.
A compassionate roll:
we must be done
with cruelty
especially to ourselves,
to start again
beaming like the sun;
fresh.
But a roll that shows
we've reached the end
of polite moves to
repair and re-create the Earth,
and will press hard
on any parts of us
even those we've loved,
that insist
on remaining
oblivious
and
asleep.

Lodestar

Here is what I believe
will be the hardest thing
to do:
to remember
that we have
a soul.
It is so quiet
the soul
and weighs
almost nothing.
It might flash
across
our dullest days
only once or twice
in a lifetime.
That it is there:
just the certainty
of knowing
must be
our lodestar.

Ancestors Never Sleep

Ancestors never sleep
and always seem to know
what they're doing.
How is this possible?
I ask myself.
Sometimes I am weary
enough to expire—
what a relief
I will think. No more obsessing
about this madness;
whatever it might be
this year, or even this century.
But ancestors merely
yawn
and send me off
for a nap.
Not only is life not over,
they sniff,
it has barely begun for you.
There are eternities
waiting just beyond
the next bad movie
you fear you'll be
starring in.
Go to sleep. Rest your brain.
Rest your heart. Rest your eyes
and all your thoughts.
We have been with you
from the beginning
which didn't exist
and we will be with you
until that moment of
nonexistence
swings round again.
You are attempting to carry
the suffering
all around you

but your back is bending.
Let us bear it for you.
Knowing as we do
that it is only
a difficult turn
on a never ending
journey
of dissolving
and becoming
and dissolving
again
and becoming
once more;
forever & ever
on
and
on.
Save despair,
our beloved
sweetcakes,
for a couple of eons
later.

Especially to the Toddlers of Iran (and Other Countries)
And Those Just Learning to Ride Bikes

It is the well-being
of your country
so far
away
I may
only have
been there
in
my dreams
that
lets
me
sleep
at
night.

The Future Captured in a Heartless Fist

Somehow it is left to us
this most hopeful of generations
to bear
the unbearable.
We do not need to have given birth
to the children
who are being destroyed
to know they are our children
not only in the present and the past
but certainly in the future.
All children are connected at birth
to all the others ever to arrive.
Their faces turned upward
toward the parents all grown-ups were meant to be.
How can you separate your child
from mine?
Little one, they have captured you
and placed you in a cage.
What are we to make of this?
Are we supposed to see you
as an animal?
Though animals also do not deserve
this fate.
Are we supposed to think
that you are, at five years old,
already a "terrorist"?
Are we to believe you deserve
to stand alone in this tiny jail
obviously constructed with you in mind
while grown-ups stand around
and frighten you?
Who paid for this cage
anyway?
Whose taxes?
Whose labor?
Whose sweat?
Little One,

you are Palestinian
you are also Earthling,
you are Every Child.
By most humans of this planet
you are beloved.
But in this moment,
so hard to own
as what any parent or grown-up
anywhere
could desire or wish
you are The Future
captured in a heartless
fist.

Julian

Julian Bond, 1940-2015

The first time I sang
"We Shall Overcome"
was in a circle
on the lawn of Trevor Arnett Library
at Atlanta University
and by chance
I was holding
your hand.
We were all so young,
Julian,
and so hopeful
in our solidarity.
I stumbled over some of the words
in the new to me
song
but you sang solemnly,
correctly,
devoutly,
believing every word
you sang
with your whole
handsome
heart.
A friend writes
that you will be buried
at sea
and I nod
because that is how it felt
those years so long ago;
that we were so young,
vulnerable,
swimming against
an awesome tide of hatred
and despair
definitely
at sea.

But we persevered
as so many waves
mountains of tears
came roaring toward, and over, us.
Martin, Jack, Bobby,
Fannie Lou
who never said what else
they did to her
after they beat her
body into a leathery
stiffness
after arresting her in
that small town jail.
Julian,
the guns,
the drugs,
the miseducation,
also aimed at all we loved.
And us somehow
you somehow
managing to keep
standing.
You were so young
in those days
of tight jeans
and a young wife
"the other Alice"
I thought of her.
She who would save
your life
when we thought you'd
lost it.
They are saying many things
about you now
so much praise
that is well earned.
And yet,
I wonder if they can
imagine

the young man you were
standing in
that Circle of Life
so long ago
holding hands
with those as fragile,
as determined,
as pure as you
waiting for the future
we would make
with just our circle
and our song.

The Dancing Shack

for Alice from Beverly Buchanan
Beverly Buchanan, Artist, 1940–2015

Someone who knew me well
and that I'd lived
in many a gray shack
my mother transformed
with flowers
took me to your house
to meet you:
to see the shacks
you rescued from our shame
and transformed with your wit,
small nails, old boards,
and paint.
I was enchanted to see
my mother's magic
emerge
from the end
of your brush.
Now you have left us. The streaming
light through all your shacks'
cracks
like the streaming genius
of your own obsessed mind.
How do we make new
and restorative of soul
the old pain? How do we learn
to carry with grace and humor
all that has happened to us?
Buchanan, for instance. Whose name
was that before it was slapped across
the memory of the enslaved?
Your ancestors
in Africa were not Buchanans
and may have been esteemed artists
every one of them,

for all we know.
Ah, Beverly,
all of us in our age clan
are in the homestretch now.
We will not be far behind you.
Trailing our chalk, our pencil sticks
with which we wrote and drew in the dirt,
our paints made from berries, barks,
and tears.
With open hands
we have offered our art
made from whatever scraps
were left over from our destruction,
their absence from
the big house table of greed and ignorance
never missed.
This poem is to say how glad I am
to have the shack
you made for me. Red as a strawberry!
I would never have thought of that; yet
how right it has turned out to be.
For I do not wallow in sadness
though it visits more often these days
than I would like;
the world is dying
in so many ugly ways
and humans with it.
And yet, against all odds
I realize
there will always be a Beverly Buchanan
arising from a virtual "nowhere"
to cobble together the broken pieces
—left over from the beauty
that is destroyed—
and paint them red
for dancing.

The Circle

I myself do not believe
in political parties
comprised, generally, in my experience, of so
many who
are not awake. Still, all options must be
presented by those who care.

An unbalanced wakefulness
can be as treasonous
as blind sleep.

Let there be a private counsel
first
with one's own heart.
One's own bright
or blighted
spirit and soul.

Then from that sacred spot
of personal centering
move outward
to The Circle.

There are always others
more wise than us.
Let us hear them with humility
and do not, as in the past,
obey an impulse
to shout them down.

We owe it to all the others
gone before us
black, white, red;
you know,
the merry ones
who would have died
laughing—

if this cheekiness
had not been
crushed out of them—
to step thoughtfully here
into what future
there is left.

We have not lost
and are not lost
if we hold ourselves
in honor and respect.

There is a way forward
and yes
it is with a broken
heart
but it is our own way
collectively convened,
pondered,
shared.
The Circle (call all your friends!),
like the church
in all our struggles
an extension
of our unshakably
trustworthy
and consoling
arms.

Like a wise grandparent
who loves us
more than life itself
The Circle sends us out
into the world
in the direction we choose
fortified
by its collective wisdom
and ancestor driven
love.

The King Has Gone Away for Good: Long Live the King!

Imagine, B.B. King,
I have listened to you and Lucille
my whole life.
Sometimes when I have had the blues
I have listened to you
and thought:
it can't be all bad;
I am on the planet while *he* is here too
and he is singing!

It is hard to take
this leaving of us
that you have done.
And yet, how tired,
how exhausted
you must be. Singing
to us all these years.
And what did you eat,
I wonder, pondering your
portliness;
especially in the early days;
and at the back doors
of how many "respectable
establishments"?

You know that word
"irrepressible"
that describes the joy
and pain of our resistance
to dullness, giving up,
wearing out? That is how
I've thought of you. Who knew
what kept you going? Except
a spirit that refused surrender
to despair.

———

When she was three or four
I took my daughter
to hear you sing
in Mississippi. You were
"amazing," my favorite word
and observation
about this Life.
And you, large and dark
and radiant with your special
brand of unstoppable joy
kissed her warm delighted
cheek
and smiled at her father
and me, outlaws in that land,
as we stood in awe.

This painting by Sherard Van Dyke
I encountered one day
in her studio in Amsterdam. You were on one easel
Billie Holiday on another.
I could afford to buy one
painting.
I chose Billie but the painting of you never left
my heart. Twelve years later (or something
like that) I called Van Dyke
and she remembered perfectly
how much I had wanted you.
Guess what, she said, when I said
at last I could afford the Green B.B.,
I still have it!

And so you came across the ocean,
Across the continent. Across my living
room to rest
where I can see you
every day. The greenness
of your skin "testifying"
—a word you liked—

to your supreme
earthiness.

Thank you for being here
while I am here, while we
are here, Radiant Soul.
Thank you for guidance,
truth, honesty, passion,
sincerity (most beautiful of all charms,
I've found)
thank you for your special darkness
that illuminates both shadow and light. Magic.

All those days and nights
on the road
you gave all you had,
your way
of dying wealthy.

Thank you for the teaching.

Welcome to the Picnic

I can never banish the image
of you, manacled, between two psychopaths
being marched to a defenseless
beating
that will leave your brain injured.
Try as I might, your lonely walk,
blind justice not even stumbling
behind
or anywhere in the neighborhood
will forever haunt me:
as you face two, three, four,
a dozen
soulless creatures
who enjoy beating you
to the ground; when your hands are not only tied,
but, demonstrating their true courage,
fastened behind your back.
Of what are we reminded:
the enslaved men worked to death
in seven years
their heads bashed in
when they could no longer work
their bodies, their bones, turning up
white with time; and directly underneath
where they fell: Where, but Wall Street.
Or the plantations
and hundreds of years of this.
Beatings. Beatings to death.
Beatings to incontinence. Beatings to brain damage.
A friend tells me she never uses the word
"picnic" for this very reason: it reminds her that the mothers
and fathers and brothers and children of the psychopaths
came to the beating, hanging, quartering
eviscerations or whatever else could be imagined
to entertain at a lynching
and brought baskets of food
to enjoy with the show. The torture of the Pickaninny

the word that to her sounds too much like "picnic"
and was often used for the victim
whatever his or her age
was the eagerly anticipated attraction.
If they were lucky, these picnicking families, they
got to take home trophies. Trophies sometimes seared from
the flames. Fingers, ears, toes.
A foot. Remember how DuBois saw those human feet in a
butcher's window in downtown Atlanta?
Brother, Sister, Children,
you are not crazy to feel crazy
here.
Understanding this, may you realize
a greater exterior calm
and an unshakeable inner peace. We have lived within the soul
of brutality from the beginning of our connections here.
The harshness of knowing our journey
could easily steal our joy. To learn not to extend
our disaster!
That is what teachers
are for.

The Lesson

They are crazy. That was the answer
we received as children as we wondered why?
Why did they abuse, mistreat, slander, degrade,
why did they lynch, murder, kill. Was there no feeling of shame or
    sadness
no tickling of remorse?
They are sick. Our grandmothers said. Then, no,
they are not just sick. Sickness we might cure
with herbs.
They are crazy. This might only be cured
with isolation but there are so many and they are everywhere.
I was so little I could see reality: So are we so many, Grandmama, I
    offered,
we too, are everywhere.

All the Fast Car Ads Look Crazy Now

Do you notice how all
the fast car ads look
crazy now?
There she is, blonde,
hair color (if from a bottle)
polluting the environment
and affecting her brain
but copied by some of the most
brainwashed though
intelligent
people on the planet
who used to actually enjoy
the multi-colors and multi-fuzzies
of their own hair.
His hair is darker. Always.
Why is this? Is he attempting
to pass off his suspect
DNA
as belonging
to the "free" world?
Suppose she's really poor
though?
Suppose his real job
was shipped to China.
It doesn't seem to matter
in the ads.
It's what you're made
to think of:
somewhere there are free
people:
they are laughing;
they are happy;
they are blonde
and the dark-haired man
is hoping at least
his children will be.
What madness is this?

They go careening across your screen
laughing.
They never seem to think
about Chernobyl
and the warehoused defective
children in Russia
and Scandinavia.
Nor do they appear worried
about Fukushima
and the plumes of radiation
in air and ocean
eating California,
Canada and Mexico.
They are laughing,
the car they drive is fast.
They are fast.
All is well in their world.
The ad is meant to sell you their
security.
That world of freedom, speed,
and lack of care,
is meant to seem large.
But really it is
no bigger than your screen.
Turn it off.
Attend to your motorbike,
the broken lamppost outside
your window,
the rubbish
despoiling
the beauty
of your slow
but larger than screen size
village
street.

Light a Candle

for Raif Badawi

The Saudi Arabian government ordered one thousand lashings and ten
years in prison to Raif Badawi for "insulting Islam."

Darkness is gaining.
Winter in Gaza.
Babies freeze to death.
Soldiers shoot children
aiming for their eyes.
Light a candle for us all.
Light a candle for the children.
Light a candle for blind justice.
Light a candle
for the death
of hope
in Saudi Arabia.
And though it is hard
to look
and harder to let ourselves
feel:
thinking: What can
I do?
Light a candle
and say a prayer
for this man.

My 12-12-12
Zapata, Mexico

They told us we must be ready
before dawn
and just at dawn
Manuel came for us.
We rode in silence as the day
was breaking
to join
a slowly building crowd
of people
on the outskirts
of Zapata.
There are so many Zapatas in Mexico.
And many Villas
it must be said.
But there we were
a small contingent
waiting for Her.
A nun showed up first,
of course,
this being hundreds of years
later.
I liked her though; she led us
in song.
And soon, sure enough,
She appeared.
Brown, slender,
somber and very young,
maybe still languid
from interrupted sleep,
this year's incarnation
of La Virgen de Guadalupe.
Shivering a bit
in the morning chill
she wrapped her green mantle
that tended to slip
more securely over her

loving head. With the help
of many hands,
her neighbors
and friends,
she climbed into the back
of the waiting
pickup truck.
I could have started weeping
right there. But no, I held on.
Though happiness and love welled up
behind my eyelids.
They have survived, I thought.
As the marchers, and we,
my companion and me,
fell in
behind the truck.

Our nun singing and chanting
and the two of us
humming the parts
of litany
(most of them)
we did not understand.
Hail Mary, Full of Grace
pray for us now
and in the hour
of our death.
The only thing
we thoroughly understood
chanted
and hoped
would also, at death,
apply to us!
We began to walk.
It was only three or four miles.
We crossed a river.
We saw early morning dairymen
in the brush
milking cows.

We saw fields and hills
of this most beautiful part
of beautiful Mexico.
The Virgen led us
faithfully. So young, so brown, so long of dark hair.
Her face only twice breaking into a smile
that showered us, walking behind Her,
with Her radiance.
The sun appeared only briefly,
the day was still, overcast
and calm.

Yes, we ended up,
the truck and all
of us, outside a convent
where the nun and the priest
were waiting.
But the ceremony
linking the Virgens
Mary and La Señora de Guadalupe
occurred
in Nature
outside
beneath sheltering trees.
And this also
moved my heart. For I am more
at home with the other Her,
the one who creates
the out of doors
so casually.

We sang, and hummed,
stood and sat
(chairs materializing behind us
out of thin air)
until the last song,
then turned
to retrace our steps.
Sore in thigh and foot

but fulfilled.
Halfway back
we recrossed the river
which
unusual for this time of year
was full of water.
I sat, fanning myself, on the railing of the bridge.
I am inside the picture now,
I said to my companion
who feared I might fall.
I did not care, really,
but assured
him
I am more careful of my life
than it might appear. I recognize
the gift it is to me; out of gratitude
I protect it.
Yes, I am inside the picture now,
not just looking
at the painting.
And I thought of this
while trudging down a once unknown road
in the heart of Mexico
that I now know very well;
feeling joy and relief
to see another Virgen
my Mexican sister
Yolanda
speeding toward us
in her new Pathfinder
coming with cool water
and delicious
fresh papaya
to rescue all of us
and, smiling, deliver me.

And in the Red Box

for Obenewa, African daughter, at Christmas

And in the red box
tied with red ribbons
tell me justice lies
and schoolbooks for children
tell me there is
a sandwich
for the man
starving
on the corner.
Tell me when Christmas
comes
peace
and a warm fire
happiness
and
joy
an end
to selfishness
comes with it.

You Were Sixteen

You were sixteen
and on your way to pick up
your birthday
cake.

My partner offers
photographs
of your battered
head
that I cannot
view.

You have died under the blows.

Look at the soldier
he says
when he sees
my eyes
are turning away:
sixteen too,
perhaps.
Dressed in the olive
drab
of her country's
police; too young
to imagine
as she poses
above her kill
that she has murdered
a dream of youth
that will haunt
her
her whole life.

Fullness of Heart

*for the people of Bab Al Shams, Gate of the Sun encampment
in Palestine*

We will never regret
having been born in this
cruel time
for we recognize it
for what it is: the time of fullness
of heart.
When the heart, on a daily basis
fills to capacity
and overflows
with love
of the people:
of the people's
children, throwing stones against tanks,
of the people's women
combatting erasure;
of the people's men
risking all
for dignity
and peace.

Fullness of heart.

What is fullness of heart
but a heart
filled
a throat filled
eyes filled
with tears?
Tears we do not regret
because we the people
of the world
are standing fast
together
at last
on Palestine.

Who knows what will happen next?
Craziness has a long shelf life.
All we do know
is now is the time
to live life to the full
and without
regret.

I speak for myself
and I believe also
for you.
Standing fast
together at last.
For Palestine.
Our tears
no less than our blood
our glue.

Aloisea Inyumba, Presente

Aloisea, my younger sister,
it was love at first sight.
For there you stood
in the garden of the presidential
compound
along with its sister occupant
and you were both giggling
like Spelman girls
at a Morehouse tea.
I saw in you my roommate
from Uganda
with her proud and honest
gaze;
her stoic lack
of pretension:
I saw my other classmates
from Kenya, Tanganyika
Sierra Leone
and
the always
challenged
Liberia.
Dorcas, Constance,
Mary, Caroline.
Not their real names
at all; though I would not
understand this until much later.
Aloisea Inyumba,
you were able to keep,
to live under,
to offer
with your wise and fearless eyes
who you really were.
For this, we black Americans
might have envied you.
But love of your free look
would demolish this.

And you were so clear!
As we poked into orphanages
and dim and dusty huts
filled with the malnourished
whom you vowed
to feed and properly shelter:
This misery is not part of Rwanda's dream,
you said. *We will change it!*
You showed me places and shared experiences
I could not believe
could actually exist.
A woman's answer to the question
of homeless people
especially homeless children
is to take them
into one's home.
Children were not meant
to live in orphanages. There seemed no doubt
in your mind
about this.

Aloisea Inyumba.
You were the most beautiful
of all the beauties
I witnessed
in your beautiful country.
Zainab, our friend,
also a stellar warrior
for the good of women and children
and by their inclusion
in the health of the world,
also a warrior for the good
of men,
told me of your death.

All I could think of at that moment
was: *This too? How can we bear it?*
I was so undone to hear this news I could not weep
until now.

For I remembered not only your tireless work
for your people and your loyalty to your
friends who worked beside you, whether in high places
or in low,
I recalled your generosity.
Alice, you said,
when I said to you: I love Rwanda!
Come back and live here.
I laughed.
No, you said, in all seriousness:
Come back. You are home here.
And I tell you what: When you come back
I will see to it that you are given a plot of land
to grow your garden on
and, you said smiling impishly,
best of all,
we will give you cows!
Cows!
Another love of my life, as, apparently,
they are the love of the lives
of many Rwandans.

What is the dream, Aloisea?
Let us make it clear again,
as the world reawakens
to possibilities
until now
barely thought:
Is it the peaceful nation
in which every child is wanted
and adored;
where every woman
has a voice?
Where every man's dignity
is rooted in nonviolence?

Oh, my beloved sister,
to walk with you in a garden
of collards and tomatoes,

to rest on a hillside in Rwanda
flanked by our cows . . .
Bliss.
Other women of Africa
will live this dream
after us.
But it is you who
in your brief years
saved it
shining
for us all.

Rest in *Well Done*, beloved sister
of our clan. Aloisea Inyumba:
Minister of Gender and Family;
Kigali, Rwanda.

I Confess I Do Not Understand the Mind That Needs to Cause This Suffering

for Nurit Peled who sent me the photograph Palestinians Going to Work—Morning Routine

I confess
I do not understand the mind
that needs to cause this: Palestinian workers
herded like cattle
in a long line
to their places of ill paid
employment.
How happy can you make yourself by
causing this suffering?
How long can you sleep
as morning comes
and you pretend they are not
trudging
your way?
Withstanding insults
so many to a mile.
Cold
hungry
unimaginably poor.

Nauseated
from grief
and fear
but trudging desperately
onward.
For the people
for the kids
for the pride of being
who they are now and were before.
Never stopping.
Trudging onward:
toward the frigid
welcome
of your back door.

Not from Here

(from *Chitauri Blues,* a work in progress)
for beloved Kaleo who opened this door to me

Anybody who despises elephants except for their tusks
is not from here.
Anybody who decapitates mountains
is not from here.

Anybody who assassinates
rivers, oceans,
and the air,
is not from here.

Anybody who "disappears" continents
of buffalo
and foxes, turtles and rain forests
oil, gold, diamonds
and sandalwood
is not from here.

You can sleep on
if you like.

But this is the easiest way
to tell
who is not Earthling.

Stop
nodding off
about this.

(The big-time drug dealers,
pulling global strings,
not the teenagers with their
pitiful
nickel bags,
are not from here.)
——

Earthlings
see grass
(Chiefs Joseph and Seattle
for example)
as hair
on the Mother's head
rocks
as her bone
and teeth.

Oil and water
as her blood and sweat.
Veins of gold
as her meridians.

Diamonds her tears
of stress,

sandalwood her perfume.

The Earthling
has her feet on the
Mother's shoulders
gratefully.

She is not from out *there*
(Where the concept of Mother might not even exist.)
She knows
she is
from here.

They have removed us
almost completely
from our own minds
our souls
and from our defenseless
—because of this
fatal absence—
planet.

We are in swoon.

The snack we are to them
has no need of consciousness.

The ones who are
from *there*.

But let us take our stand
nonetheless
as Earthlings:
we are from here
and
on awakening
let us resolve not
to fall asleep again
or forget
that to protect
Mother Earth
(and Father Sky
who is also under
attack)
is to protect
us all
who are
from here.

Cosmic locals
who refuse to have
our obscure, back galaxy
Paradise
raped, trashed and
cannibalized
before our
stricken
eyes
by cosmic tourists.

I Am Telling You, Discouraged One, We Will Win

I am telling you
Discouraged One
we will win.
And I will show you
why.
We are the offspring
of the ignorantly
discarded:
we conjure
sunrise
with our smiles
and provoke music
out of trash.
Who can completely
disappear
such genius?

This is why humanity
is worth
loving.
Fiercely.
Passionately.
Without a moment
of holding back.
I used to think
it was only
Africans
I loved so dangerously
then I thought it was
Indians;
then Mexicans
Vietnamese
Guatemalans
Cambodians
Laotians
Nicaraguans
Cubans

Haitians
Salvadorans . . .
all
those dear ones
so endlessly
lied about.
But no, it is all of us.
It is humanity.
We are special.
If you don't believe me
take the time to awaken
and truly witness
yourself.

We Are Never Without Help

A Poem for Celia Sánchez

We are never without help.
Look for it always
to surprise you.
There is no end to the joy
of discovery
just as there is no end
to amazement.
Those who give their lives
for truth and bread
for the triumphant
flash of a vivid
bougainvillea
even as they
die
in unspeakable
ways
or whose last notice
is of a simple daisy
still striving
in a corner
across
a drying lawn
have never taken
their arms
away
never taken
them away
from being
around us.

The Good Ones

for Hugo Chávez, Presente

The good ones
who listen
to women
to children and the poor
die too soon,
their lives bedeviled
by opposition:
our hearts grieve for them.

This was the world my father knew.

A poor man
he saw good men come and mostly go;
leaving behind
the stranded and bereft.
People of hopes, dreams, and so much
hard work!
Yearning for a future
suddenly
foreclosed.

But today
you write me all is well
even though the admirable
Hugo Chávez
has died this afternoon.

Never again will we hear that voice
of reasoned anger
and disgust
of passionate vision
and of triumph.

This is true.

———

But what a lot he did in his 58 years!
you say.
What a mighty ruckus
Hugo Chávez made!

This is also true.

Thank you for reminding me.

That though life—
this never-ending loop—
has passed us by today
but carried off
in death
a hero
of the masses
it is his spirit
of fiercely outspoken
*cariño**
that is not lost.

That inheritance
has gone instantly
into the people
to whom he listened
and it is there
that we will expect it
to rise
as early as
tomorrow;
and there
that
we will encounter it
always
soon again.

affection

What Does It Take to Be Happy?

for Stephane Hessel, who seemed to know

Even on those days
the news is fully bad.
And all you can do is get out of bed
and failing that
give thanks you have a bed not to get out of.
What does it take to make us smile
when we feel the sword of anger
and hatred
sharp against the backs
of our peaceful necks?
What does it take
to make us stand together
as if we just grew that way?
What does it take to know
the day of peace and justice
will one day come?
No matter who
is so badly
directing traffic?
What does it take
to feel a joy so strong
you can almost levitate?
All it takes, really,
is presence,
knowing that you, and those who feel
as you do,
ignoring roadblocks
will arrive.
Will brave the flights, the slights,
the nights of wondering
if and why:
the years of pain sometimes required
to know
where it is most essential
to appear.

Later We Would Miss You So Much

for Chelsea Manning

Later we would miss you
so much.
But on that day
we had you with us
& we were *so*
with you.
Your happiness,
of a man
knowing he was
on his way
to glory
to being shot down;
a man beaming
with triumph
to see us
the advancing crowds,
caused us to cheer inwardly
in response to every
word.

Later we would recall
for our children
and grandchildren
the thrill of being
in your presence
as you rose
to meet your day.
You were so happy!
Let us not forget that.
Fear, doubt, the most horrible
criticisms evil genius
could devise
had not stood
finally
or at all
against your love.

———

Even the white people
that day
looked different
to us
who had never known them
in their free form.
They had a look
of release
of knowing they were bound also
by chains and shackles
& were at last
shaking themselves free.

Perched in a tree
better to see & hear
grateful for the tree's
rustling witness
on that fateful day
& meticulously careful
not to harm
its leafy offering
of vantage point (it would later be cut down, of course).
I lived the long moment
of your address to us
to the full.

They would edit and condense
it later
to dull our memory
and your impact
to make it, and you, more manageable
for them.
But we were not deceived.
You were brilliant
and your message never confined

only to dreams
though you were only a few

short years away
from your death
at 39.

What did you give us,
Martin, at such sacrifice
to yourself?

After 50 years
of pondering the gift
of your life
I know you gave us
Consciousness
of our inalienable
rights
as beings not only
of our country (a mystery in itself)
but more importantly
of our Universe.
And beyond that
you showered us, our wounded and weakened
psyches,
with your example
of fearless love.

Fearless love for those beyond
immediate family
& friends
is very rare.
But you had it.

I think the Beings
who destroyed
your body
felt,
looking at you,
that they'd been robbed,
shortchanged.
How could you

a mere black preacher's
son
possess the gold
that eluded them;
gold, for all their digging
all over the earth,
they'd never have?

Not only that:
Martin, Beloved,
you ran the race
for Love
and won it.
We know this
for sure
50 years later.

No longer the girls & boys
of 18 & 19
arriving at the March
on cheap buses
from all over
the place—
We know it, Martin,
by our own devotion to life,
to each other,
to forests, rivers, and trees that support us
through every devastation,
by our cheering of every
young voice
that raises the bar of love
to your standard;
we know it by our gratitude
Martin.
We know it by our faith,
not in leaders
but in our belief that love
can overcome our fears.
———

Finally, Martin:
after all the dry years
of bearing your memory
most often
in silence,
We know it
by our tears.

Necks of Clay

Someone said to me:
Oh, stop that! He has feet
of clay.
This person's clay
went to the neck.
Can we listen to imperfect
humans?
I've always preferred them
myself.
Does this make us mad?
Can we hear our own
small voices
muffled by
the mud
of being:
pleading
for release?

Who the Annunaki Saw?

Tiny Mother,
I knew you had to exist
behind all the lies
about you.
I knew you would live
somewhere fresh
wild
with the sun dancing
with your earth colored skin.
I knew you would adorn yourself
with whatever struck your fancy.
That it would feel natural
for you
to be part of the All.
Oh, Small Mother.
Today we miss you so very much!
Your ease among all expressions
of the real;
your delight in style
that is never lost
on the heart
that is free.
When the strange beings
from somewhere else
first approached you
did you try to show them
how easy
even splendid
it can be
to live on Earth?
And did they refuse
to hear you—
as they still refuse?
Are you who the Annunaki saw?
Did they have the sense
at least
to be charmed

as we are,
all these eons later?
Or did they cause that look
in your eyes
that so pains
me today;
a distant daughter
held in troubled enchantment
by your amazing
face?
In my house you hang
in a place of honor
so that I see you
every day.
It is a face that has lasted.
But whose spirit now, I see it in your look,
is deeply challenged.
Endangered.
Small Mother, sister, ancestor, aunt,
thank you for showing us
the face of a true
earth being;
someone who knows
no separation
of beauty
and self.

from *Chitauri Blues,* a work in progress

The photograph of a woman among the Omo people is by German
photographer Hans Silvester. It was given to me by a beloved sister, in
whose house hangs another beautifully adorned "Small Mother."

Inner Landscape

for S and C

We have not seen each other
in over a decade;
your son is very tall, you say,
your daughter, learning
to ride horses.
Later, savoring our chance meeting
in the local ice-cream store
I look about the land
and see evidence of your helpfulness
everywhere:
the big sister
sycamore tree
the one that remains of three saplings
you brought to my housewarming
on such a big truck
now shades, even shadows
my house.
The slope above the pond
that you planted with trees
is now a forest
that keeps the hillside
from sliding down.
The pond
that leaked so mysteriously
is now stable and shining;
I swim there each day
while dreaming of walnuts
and pecans
and persimmons
and grapes
still to come
in due season.

Today you send to my house
boxes of peaches,
cartons of blueberries

a shocking abundance!
My guests
who have never known the peach
as I grew up knowing it
in Georgia
are mesmerized by the sight
the scent
the texture
the flavor
of each one they sink
happy teeth
into.
We lie about in ecstasy
moaning
our delight.

Thank you, my friends,
who
so many years ago,
brought back to me
from sobering
travels
a solitary small tree
from far away
and very troubled
Chiapas.
It stands tall now
in a circle
of wisteria
Chardonnay
grapevines
and a wispy plant with
crimson plumes
whose name
I cannot
at this moment
recall. Though I always think
of you
when I see it.

This tree,
so far from its home
reminds me
of neighbors,
of friends,
of the welcome we can
sometimes be
for each other
or find
among strangers;
the welcome of simple
planting, and digging,
eating,
sharing whatever
in the world
is going on
treasuring the delicious
goodness
of an unexpected
moment of happiness
that changes the inner landscape
forever.

Recommended: "Georgia on My Mind" by Ray Charles

Hope Is a Woman Who Has Lost Her Fear

for Sundus Shaker Saleh, Iraqi mother, with my love

In our despair that justice is slow
we sit with heads bowed
wondering
how
even whether
we will ever be healed.

Perhaps it is a question
only the ravaged
the violated
seriously ask.
And is that not now
almost all of us?
But hope is on the way.

As usual Hope is a woman
herding her children
around her
all she retains of who
she was; as usual
except for her kids
she has lost almost everything.

Hope is a woman who has lost her fear.
Along with her home, her employment, her parents,
her olive trees, her grapes. The peace of independence;
the reassuring noises of ordinary neighbors.

Hope rises, She always does,
did we fail to notice this in all the stories
they've tried to suppress?
Hope rises,
and she puts on her same
unfashionable threadbare cloak
and, penniless, she flings herself
against the cold, polished, protective chain mail

of the very powerful
the very rich—chain mail that mimics
suspiciously silver coins
and lizard scales—
and all she has to fight with is the reality of what was done to her;
to her country; her people; her children;
her home.
All she has as armor is what she has learned
must *never* be done.
Not in the name of War
and especially never in the
name of Peace.

Hope is always the teacher
with the toughest homework.

Our assignment: to grasp
what has never been breathed in our stolen
Empire
on the hill:

Without justice, we will never
be healed.

For more information about the inspiring courage of this mother of five,
visit codepink.org.

Sweet People Are Everywhere

for Young Bryon, Who Is Getting a Passport

Some of the people in Turkey
are very sweet.
Some of those in Afghanistan
are very sweet.
Some of the people in the Americas
are very sweet.
In Canada too
some of the people
are sweet.
In Mexico
you will definitely find
sweet people.
Likewise
in the Sudan.
There are sweet people
among the Zulu
in South Africa
and every language group in Africa
has some sweet people
in it.
There are sweet people
in Iceland
and
in Russia.

There are many sweet people in Korea.
There are millions of sweet people in China.
There are sweet people in Japan.
If the sweet people were the leaders in these historically warring
    Asian countries
they would treat each other
much better!
There are sweet people
in the Congo.
There are sweet people
in Egypt;

and sweet people
in Australia.
Many sweet people are
in Norway.
Numerous sweet people are
in Spain.
There are many sweet people
in Ghana
and Kenya
and sweet people also
in Guam
and the Philippines.
There are sweet people
in Cuba.
Many sweet people
exist in Iran.
There are sweet people
in Libya and Colombia.
Sweet people are
in Vietnam.
Sweet people exist
in England and Burma.
There are sweet people
for sure
in Ireland.
Sweet people are
in France.
Sweet people are holding on
in Syria.
They are doing the same
in Iraq.
Some sweet people live
in Venezuela.
Many very sweet people
live in Brazil.
There are sweet people
in Israel
as there are sweet people

also
in Palestine.

Actually, in almost every house
on the planet
there is at least one
very sweet person
that you would be happy to know.

Sweet people are everywhere!

Being sweet, they must not be disappeared.
We are lost
if we can no longer experience
how sweet human beings can be.

Promise me never
to forget this.
No matter how far
you go
on this new passport,
where you are directed to land
your own sweet self
or who sends you.

And When They Spy on Us

for Snowden

And when they spy
on us
let them discover
us
loving—
it really doesn't
matter what we are loving
let it be
an exercise
of the heart.
You can begin
with
your car—
if that has been
your training.
After all
the great ones
tell us
it is all about
and by any means
necessary
opening the heart.
It could be
your dog—
that is where
most of my friends
and I
would be found.
It could be
desert
or mountain
river
or a peculiar
bend
in a lonely road
that makes you

ache
with longing.
Let them find us
deep in
the conspiracy
(breathing together)
of love—
our hearts open;
resigned to being
these
sometimes ridiculous
and always vulnerable
human beings
that those
who have no
experience that
love can exist
in this world
must spy
upon.

Confident Anticipation of Joy

How peculiar it feels
to speak about
health care in America
taking care of people's
health
while our government
bombs
the limbs
off children
in faraway lands.
And starves and imprisons
not a few of them
at home.
How odd
that it seems
not obviously known
that true health care
must mean, at minimum,
deliberate non-harming
of anyone?
How strange is haggling
over how much this or that
medical
"procedure"
is going to cost;
meaning strictly
where our own bodies
and they *are* precious
are concerned.
While over there
military
"procedures"
our country exports
may
slice a grandfather
in half while his
grandchildren

who have crowded
around him
in
confident anticipation
of joy
become clots of blood
and matted hair
on the walls.
What's left of the walls.
Weird how we talk
and haggle
as if we are the only
people in the Universe
needing
care of our health.
Health care:
care of Life
itself.
What the maimed
and slaughtered
in many lands
have died,
hopelessly
crying for.

The Mother of Trees

If I could be
the mother of Wind
I would blow all fear
away from you.

If I could be
the mother of Water
I would wash out the path
that frightens you.

If I were the mother
of Trees
I would plant
my tallest children
around your feet
that you might
climb
beyond all danger.

But alas,
I am only
a mother of humans
whose magic powers
have vanished
since we allow
our littlest ones
to face injustice
suffering
& the unholiest
of terrors
alone.

Note: This disturbing photograph of a small child being arrested by
soldiers three times his size was sent to me by the great Israeli peace
activist and humanitarian Nurit Peled-Elhanan, who lost her daughter in a
suicide bombing. There was an explanation of what was happening in the

photograph—a war on children who threw stones at the tanks demolishing their homes—and a request that I circulate the image. For weeks I did nothing but think about this child and all the Palestinian children taken from their schools and homes, their beds, often in the middle of the night. What is it about certain photographs? There are for most of us two or three that will not go away. Two others for me: the one of the African child slowly dying of starvation while a vulture waits within the frame; the one of John Kennedy laid out on a table in Texas, his wounds visible, especially the one near his throat, his eyes wide open. He seems shockingly young, vulnerable and precious, lying there; emblematic of the awakening leader who is always sacrificed in the long history of stillborn Americas.

Never Pass Up an Opportunity to Kiss

*Especially for our daughters and their families
in Nigeria*

Never pass up
an opportunity
to kiss:
the world has ended
& begun again
many times
before;
if we are to believe
the African Bible*
transcribed for
our frightened era
by Credo Mutwa.
Three deep bows.
Yes, never pass up
an opportunity
to kiss—
to say I love you!
to every leaf, flower
bug
or warlock
that catches your
fancy and/or your heart.

Never pass up
an opportunity
to kiss:
that sweet futile
but delectable
attempt
to touch &
to experience
the
most secret
Consciousness

of a Being
you may never
know.

*Ndaaba, My Children, *by Credo Mutwa*

The Iron Age, the Age of Sorrow

for Yusuf

Where do we go when we die?
the little child asked.
And the Ancient One who lives
within all little children said to her:
You go to the very same place you go to
each night when you fall asleep.
And therefore the parents of James
the beheaded one
whose face was brave and gentle and kind
are right to say he is with God
if by that they mean
the place where All That Is
resides.

Act IV The Iron Age

Act Four finds the stage of the world in total darkness, illusion and
despair. There has been an extreme decline in moral, ethical and spiritual
values. Human beings are chained to the pillars of immoral practices
and habits. Widespread sorrow and unrest have become the norm of
human experience. The world is divided into many groups, many of which
are pitted against each other in games of power conditioned by self-
interest and expediency. The human family is at a breaking point. As the
night wears on, the population explodes exponentially until the planet's
resources reach their limits.

—The Brahma Kumaris

When a Poet Dies

for Samih al-Qasim

While a poet is dying
all the trees droop their branches
not drop them
but let them hang like empty sleeves:
the sun is seen, if at all, through a mist
it made itself
from the salty water
the ocean sprays.
But when a poet dies
there is happiness in all the heavens
and in earth
and trees rustle loudly
and suns shine fiercely
and oceans roar.
That is because the poet
is journeying
at last returning
to the source of Sound
where all things forever live; the body
left behind not even a memory
to Divinities
that for so long
and mostly unnoticed
have shared
the bright path.

The Language of Bombs

Dearest Zainab,
whenever my country bombs your country,
I think of you.
Which means you are frequently on my mind.
I often think of the bombers
and how little they can see
of what is below them.
Many who returned
from earlier "missions"
said it was only later,
when they went back
and saw the ground
they bombed
that they realized
Iraqis planted
cereal grains
that covered miles
of "desert"
in brilliant green.
I think of how much you like green. And how, when you
    visit me
I make sure a window from your room looks out into
    nothing else.

It is our ignorance, Zainab,
that is killing us too
as well as your relatives
and friends.
Our teenage sons
and grandsons
especially:
shot down and left
like roadkill
in the street.

What can we say
of the madness that

has gripped our world?
The Greedy so savagely
exhibiting their starvation. So fearful
they will die of old
age
without having truly felt
—beyond bottomless hunger—
any fullness at all.

If only they could have let themselves
become acquainted
with their fear
enough to engage,
eye to eye, directly,
with the dreaded "Other."
If only they could have learned
to sit with the people
they intended to rob
and to notice, with compassion, the easily
ignitable thinness
of their clothes.
And not now speak to them
in the language of the inflated
though fatally empty man

the language of bombs.

Talking to Hamas

Huda Naim, democratically
elected official,
I do not know how it goes with you
and your children
but every day I am thinking of you.
Did you know that before we left the US
our government spokespeople
told us: you mustn't speak to anyone
from Hamas
as if we were little children
who must be warned
not to speak to strangers.
However,
the moment we heard:
someone from Hamas is here
to talk to us
every single woman
rushed to see who it was.
I had to laugh, we were so typical
in that way. One of the reasons I have enjoyed
so much
being what I am. Curious. A woman. Forgetful of advice.
And imagine our surprise
our delight,
when the dreaded "terrorist" we were warned
against—that we envisioned in battle fatigues
and shouldering a long black
rocket launcher—
turned out to be you:
portly, smiling, your eyes looking
directly into ours.
And what did we talk about: mostly
our children. Your five. Our twos and threes.
Or one. How we wanted, all of us, a sane world
for them.
Ah, Huda Naim, how I hope one day

that you will meet
our Israeli sister, Nurit, and our brother,
Miko. I know you will like them, as I do.
And the young ones refusing to join
the occupation army
but going instead
to jail
and the old ones, like Uri, somehow
holding on.
There are so many good people
in your tortured land.
And I wonder if you know
Natalya,
the poet who was with us
later
in Ramallah.
Our Natalya who writes poems to the world and emails to me
as the bombs fall around her sheltering
place: "Alice, I cannot breathe. Our hearts
have stopped."
I sit, and wring my hands,
at last old enough and sad enough,
and pathetic enough in my impotence
to do this.
Huda Naim, I pray you and your children
your whole family
all your worlds
are safe.
Yet how can it be
with Israeli bombs
and now assault rifles
and tanks
demolishing
your neighborhoods?
I would weep
but tears seem dried out
by the terror and love
I feel for you.

————

The world has awakened at last
to your true face, Huda Naim.
The world has woken
up. Though it is so used
to being asleep.
The whole world is standing, shouting its rude awakening
in the street.
That is the profit
I see, so far,
from the globally witnessed
fire sale
of your people's
pain.

Still, I have seen the world wake up
before. When it has woken up before
it has moved.

Don't Give Up (Beautiful Child, Other Self)

What they will pretend not to know
when you are injured
is how ugly you feel now.
It is hard to imagine living
without a part
of yourself.
Every other working arm or leg
or eye
or foot
no matter who owns it
will arouse your envy.
You will hate yourself
for this.
But no. There is another way
to look at all loss
and that is that it is a door.
Of course it is a door at the very bottom
of your world
but you will find it
if you stay the course
of curiosity
between who you were before
and who you now are.

It will not help much to know
what has happened to you
is happening to children
around the globe
wherever they are defenseless
and weak
wherever their protecting families
and neighbors
have already,
so many of them,
been murdered
or taken brutally away.

Nothing will penetrate your sorrow.
Or your loneliness.
This I know.
And yet
here I am singing
a song about doors
at the bottom of dark wells
stuffed already
with rats and corpses.

Here I am telling you
that in reality
and as improbable
as it may seem:
There is no (doorless)
bottom
to this life.

Gather

for Carl Dix and Cornel West

It is still hard to believe
that millions of us saw Eric Garner die.
He died with what looked like a half-dozen
heavily clad
policemen
standing on his body, twisting and crushing
him
especially his head
and neck.
He was a big man, too. They must have felt
like clumsy midgets
as they dragged him down.
Watching the video,
I was reminded of the first lynching
I, quite unintentionally, learned about:
it happened in my tiny lumber mill
town before the cows were brought in
and young white girls
on ornate floats
became dairy queens.
A big man too,
whom my parents knew,
he was attacked also by a mob
of white men (in white robes and hoods)
and battered to death
with their two-by-fours.
I must have been a toddler
overhearing my parents talk
and mystified by pieces of something
called "two by fours."
Later, building a house,
I would encounter the weight,
the heaviness, of this varying length
of wood, and begin to understand.
What is the hatred
of the big black man
or the small black man

or the medium-sized
black man
the brown man
or the red man
the yellow man
in all his sizes
that drives the white lynch mob
mentality?
I always thought it was envy:
of the sheer courage to survive
and ceaselessly resist conformity
enough to sing and dance
or orate, or say in so many outlandish
ways:
You're not the boss
of me!
Think how many black men
said that: *"Cracker,* you're not the boss*
of me";
even enslaved. Think of how
the legal lynch mob
not so very long ago
tore Nat Turner's body
in quarters
skinned him
and made "money purses"
from his "hide."
Who are these beings?
Now we are beginning to ask
the crucial question.
If it is natural to be black
and red or brown or yellow
and if it is beautiful to resist
oppression
and if it is gorgeous to be of color
and walking around free,
then where does the problem
lie?
Who are these people
that kill our children in the night?

Murder our brothers in broad daylight?
Refuse to see themselves in us
as we have strained, over centuries,
to see ourselves in them?
Perhaps we are more different
than we thought.
And does this scare us?
And what of, for instance,
those among us
who collude?
Gather.
Come see what stillness
lies now
in the people's broken
hearts.
It is the quiet force of comprehension,
of realization
of the meaning
of our ancient
and perfect
contrariness;
of what must now be understood
and done to honor
and cherish
ourselves:
no matter who
today's "bosses"
may be.
Our passion and love for ourselves
that must at last unite
and free us. As we put our sacrificed
beloveds to rest in our profound
and ample caring:
broad, ever moving, and holy,
as the sea.

*Cracker: from the crack of the whip wielded by slave drivers

Making Frittatas

for Rebecca

Ten years is a long time
and I have missed you.
I thought of this
this morning as I commenced making
a splendid (it turned out) frittata.
You taught me how to do this. After ten years during
which I assumed you did not cook—time stops
when we are absent—
you stood in my kitchen and casually,
speaking of something trivial,
made the most mouthwatering
frittata. It did not stick, it did not burn,
it was not soggy on top
it was good!
During those same ten years
I tried to make frittatas but feared they'd never cook
all the way through; all the way to the top.
But no, watching you closely, I saw
when yours threatened to remain a bit mushy
you calmly transferred it to the oven,
which I thought would surely burn it.
But—not!
Out it came the perfect consistency.
Delicious!
I was in awe.
And so, today, I think: it is all the simple
times of sharing simple things
that we have missed. The mutual teaching and learning
that is, or should be, a daughter's and a mother's right.

At the Door of Pollsmoor Prison

for Kaleo, for Madiba*

When we arrived at the door of Pollsmoor Prison
we were already deeply stirred
and sat a while outside
calming ourselves before going in. Me, breathing deeply,
you holding Madiba's image in consciousness
so that walking in you might more completely
visualize
even feel, the chains.
Once inside they showed us
the tiny cell
and placed me inside it
as they place others they wish to gift
with more than a glance at the prison experience
of the much revered, also at times much reviled,
Nelson Mandela;
I stood stretching out my arms, feeling the sides
of the cell move toward me. And feeling my whole self
listening to the eternal essence of you
that is there
and not there. I looked down
at the pallet on the floor
where you lay awake or slept so many nights
dreaming I am sure of Winnie and your girls.
There was a feeling of deep silence
in the place
where you lived for so long
and I was glad you were permitted
at least to keep
your mind.
The fashion nowadays
seems to be to rape the mind; ravage the spirit.
But there you sat or lay, night after night, and your comrades
were not so far away
in other cells.

———

What kept you going?
I think it was your love of who you were, and that you knew
who that was!
Something your jailers could not know
or even guess. They would not have known
there were rigorously
righteous elders
in your lineage
both women and men
and not only
sanusis and *sangomas***
who taught you self-respect. They would have been
ignorant of the elders' faith in you
and how much this meant to your morale.

Those who are seen, recognized, and embraced
by the wisest old people of the tribe
especially by both the women and the men
as you were
cannot really be defeated. They may be lied about,
imprisoned for decades, or even killed,
but that is not the same.

* madiba: *in Xhosa, respected elder, beloved; a term of endearment for Nelson Mandela*
** sanusi: *ancient (Zulu);* sangoma: *healer/shaman (Zulu)*

Burnt Offerings

Some realities drive us to our knees
and since I was there
already
before my altar
I unwrapped and lit
the beeswax candles
I acquired for you.
My hope is you have never heard
the story of Hansel & Gretel
the trail of bread crumbs
the witch's cages
filled with children;
the big black pot
and the cooking fat.
Never overheard elders
whisper of foreign customs
that honor
capture of children
and their sacrifice.
The lump of terror
I feel in my own heart
must be magnified
in yours.
In this cage,
seeing how many there are of you,
where would you sleep? And how?
I ask myself this, as I toss and turn.
Remembering too, the great Winnie Mandela
who endured almost a year
of solitary confinement
in a South African prison.
Three ants became her friends
as she used a bucket
like the one I see you have
for night waste (the bottom)
and for food (the lid).
When she emerged from prison

a frightfully different woman,
few South Africans
appeared to consider
the isolation, the humiliation, and the company
she had kept.
What must you think
of us, little ones?
Grownups powerless
to get you out.
What must you feel
as day by day goes by
without parents or community
(a burnt offering that perhaps you witnessed;
as fire rained from the sky)
coming to claim you?
Until
now it is only
awareness
of the
utter
brokenness
of your small lives
that regularly
comes
to visit you.

Let us consider the grown-ups who forced these children into a cage, and
send them collectively, around the planet, all our thought. Recognizing as
we do so that this was not necessarily their idea. What would we do?

A Blessing

Between those
who are old enough
and those who care
Sex is not a sin
it is a door.
Through that door
we may understand
"God"
Self
& Universe.
Passion is the great
Instructor.
Some creature
so long ago
we have forgotten
his scaly
embrace
forced us to tear ourselves
away
from what we feel
or do not feel.
Away from feeling,
or not feeling
what we know.
We will end this now.

The Prize Itself

Poem for Miko

There are many awards
that are not worth receiving;
they can be handed to you
by someone whose other hand
is stabbing you in the back.
Worse I think
is to receive an award
for bravery
from someone who is a coward
or to be given a medal
for freedom
or a prize for peace
by someone
who has no idea.
But there is the graceful
acceptance
of an award
that actually
has meaning:
when those who stand
and have stood
so closely together
against the common
danger
that the survival
of the honest
smile
between them
is the prize.
Itself.

To the Po'lice

In case you are
wondering
the answer is yes:
you have hurt us. Deeply.
Just as you
intended:
you and those
who sent you.
You do know by now
that you do not send
yourself?
I imagine your Designers
sitting back
in the shadows
laughing
as we weep.
Though usually devoid of feeling,
they are experiencing a sensation
they almost enjoy:
they get to witness, by twisted
enchantment, dozens
of strong black mothers
weeping.
They planned
and nurtured
your hatred and fear
and focused the kill shot.
Then watched you
try to explain
your innocence on TV.
It is entertainment for
them. They chuckle and drink
Watching you squirm.
They have tied you up
in a bag of confusion
from which you
will never escape.

It's true you are white, but you are so fucking poor,
and dumb, to boot, they say.
A consideration that turns
them pink
with glee.
(They have so many uses planned
for the poor, white, and dumb: you would be
amazed.)
You and the weeping mothers
have more in common than you might think:
the mothers know this.
They have known you
far longer
than you have known them. After centuries,
even those in the shadows, your masters,
offer little mystery.
If you could
find your true courage
you might risk everything
to sit within a circle, surrounded
by these women. Their eyes red
from weeping, their throats raw.
(They might strike you too, who could swear
they wouldn't?)
Their sons are dead
and it was you
who did the deed.
Scary enough.
But within that enclosure
Naked to their grief
Is where you must center
If you are ever
To be freed.

Depopulation Blues

It makes you think
of years gone by
when we dreamed
whatever we could not imagine:
but we could never, useless eaters, have dreamed or imagined
this. Maybe we could have done a better job
of imagining it
if we were different beings
and not so forgiving of the coldness
that has always been our reception
in these parts.
What could not be imagined
is how it would be done;
we knew greed and stinginess
combined would mean their elimination of us
would be
at our own expense.
Evil can be brilliant, though, it will find a way; we are not fools
completely
to be seduced by it.
Ford, Nixon, Carter,
Reagan, perhaps all
the others
knew we were counting on them
to be human as we are. Though why 800,000 Rwandans
died while we watched a televised presidential
sex scandal might have told us something. That politicians
who smiled at us and kissed our babies
blue eyes shining with triumph
well knew we were falling
into our graves
kicked by them
as they counted
our votes.

Depopulation Blues #2

They want to kill
all the world's people
simply to take what they have.
It is no longer mysterious.
We know the murders are not done
because someone is wearing
a towel.
They are not done because
there is a threat
to our sad, empty, treacherous
way of life.
Even shopping fails
to soothe us
anymore.
It is a hunger
to own that which might fill
the inside void.
But nothing can or will.

Life is being raped to death
by those who cannot
bear their inner loneliness
who cannot stop
what they cannot feel.

What Is to Be Done? Who Is to Do It?

My friend says to me:
But what can we do? Already giving up.
To be aware is already something,
I say. Consciousness rarely
leaves us unmoved. Or unmoving.
And so it is with this revelation
of what has been happening
to our children, all of them,
and especially to our boys.
The beast in so-called
civilized man
is more lethal, sinister,
grotesque and cunning
than I would have believed:
And what is it, anyhow, this beast?
How does it manifest
in every age
to plague our republic
from shadows
it projects
as light?
We are presented here
with four men who may, in their
simplicity, signal
a beginning of the end of our acute
obliviousness:
Four men sitting on metal folding chairs
talking together, almost forty years ago;
saying what they have witnessed,
what they have surmised,
what they have feared;
hearing each other out. Taping
themselves. Sharing this, all these years later,
with us, who thought we had heard it all.
This is what I believe truly grown-up men
should do. *Feel deeply*. Be present

to the steeply challenged life of the young. Care about children,
whether boys or girls, and not only about your own.
Sit together, as these
men do:
become determined
to liberate us
from our fantasy
of a society that cares:
Be resolved as Buddhas
to find a way through.
To sit a lifetime
if need be
on hard chairs.

See *Boys for Sale* on YouTube.

Banning Cruelty

Repelled by cruelty
let us ban it
from our hearts.
If we feel sad, bereft,
as if we have nothing good
to live for
think of the heart
behind these wheels—
a heart that smells
of what it carries.
Whatever else may be happening
in our perhaps blighted life:
we do not have to drive
this truck.

This truck refers to the "skunk" truck that Israel sends through Palestinian
neighborhoods spraying each dwelling with a scent of skunk.

The Energy of the Wave

for the people of Africa
(facing armored tanks and other weapons they did not make)

As a child I sensed
but did not
grasp
the power
of prayer.
It was my innocence
of the depths
that kept me unaware.
How could the passion of the heart
sent flying toward others
through humble words
change anything?
Or, rather,
what might this change?
But prayer
is an energy
that crosses mountains and deserts
and continents and seas
and is never stopped
nor even slowed
by anything.
It arrives
at its destination
as a blessing
that says: I feel—though it is but
a shadow of your sorrow—
the suffering
that has befallen
you.
Though far away,
you are securely cradled
in the safety
of my heart.
I am but a droplet
in what must become

a vast sea
to create the big wave
that washes
away
whatever demons
are harming
you.
Prayer is the beginning: when
we don't know
what else to do.
It is in this
spirit
of awareness and near impotence
beloved
kin
of butchered Africa
that we stand with you.

I Believe the Women

I believe the women.
whatever the reason
for their delay
in coming forth,
I believe they would not
come forward now
except to feel sane
and clean
again.
Sisters keep your heads up.
I also feel compassion
for the old man.
How can I not?
I love old men,
partly because
it takes so long
for them to awaken
to themselves. The selves
they hid or put to sleep
when they were five
or even younger.
Who knows what happens
to misalign a soul?
We can grow from this
if we try. It is not the end
of the world. What other people
think of us should be our last concern.
It has always been what we think of ourselves
that matters.
When we have hurt others
no matter our reason
maturity demands we own up
go to them
say I am sorry and will you forgive me?
Most people don't believe
in this
and that is why the world

is out of control.
You have lost a beloved idol
precious to you; how will you make it
without your belief?
I would walk on my knees over pebbles
to unbreak your heart.
But that is magic none of us can do.

The Slain Children of Palestine Hold Council in Paradise

Who knew death would be like this?
A young boy considers reconnecting a limb
and looks down thoughtfully
at an eye. An eye that looks
casually around Paradise
which turns out to be
everywhere.
Who knew
we would learn so much
and that the journey—
from the way things look—
will never end?
They are still fighting
and killing us
below. They do not know
we never die.
But do *they*?
And is this the way
life punishes them?
Never to be known for what
they give to the world
which is a lot:
but by what they take?
What message
to our parents
our schoolmates
our friends?
How much love they have
for us, the fallen,
how much suffering
our deaths
have caused!
If only we could drop
that feather
promised to Yoko Ono
by John Lennon!*
Announcing the promised

Realm of Being
that does not ever disappoint
or disappear!
We are the lucky ones
gone on to Glory.
How do we judge
those who murdered us?
How do we say to our families
this is not the end?
That it is Life's deathless
breath that now is
holding us,
in a peace
that has no name
or form;
inexhaustible Life
that opens once again
in dying:
Life that witnesses
everything
forever:
and is wildly flexible
in its Eternity.

* It is said that John Lennon promised his beloved Yoko that if he found whatever
"heaven" is, after his death, he would let her know by dropping a feather.

Mongers of War

Are you awake yet?
How awake are you?
Do you know what War is?
How well do you know?
Do you know how devoted
warmongers
are to War?
How they love it?
More than mothers and babies.
More than grandkids.
More than fresh water and clean soil and air.
More than mammals, birds or fish.
More than football.
More than the soccer team.
More than figs.
They appreciate
the way War shapes
& reshapes
the world
to fit their design
for people control
and planetary
mismanagement.
These mongers are meeting
in one
of their favorite dens
very soon.
Your Capitol.
Try to be there. In awareness
if not
body.
They will attempt to
Shock and Awe
into being
congressional
support
for destroying
folks just like you

in Iran;
folks you'd rather get to know.
Take a good look.
This barbarous America
red in tooth and claw
has
all along
been chewing
through the Bwana suits
of Endless Conquest.
Now
bullied into
submission
by allies
of destruction
shouting obscenities
in its ear
it desires to smother us
in grief
over yet another
greedy
tragic
ridiculous
&
altogether
backfiring
war.
Where is this going?
Not toward our dreams.
Are we awake yet?
Will we ever be?
How many more
surprised children
must die
in our sleep?

Recommended: The lyrics to Bob Dylan's "Masters of War" (1963)

To Win

(for Bob Marley's birthday, February 6)

Be what they do not want:
be thoughtful.
Be skilled at loving.
Be of good heart.
Be of the world tribe.
Who torments
the sacred
rest of us
lacks confidence
in his own
worthiness
to stand
shameless
even poor
and sing.

Morning in the Village

This morning
in the village
where I live*
I saw an old man
leisurely painting an old
two-and-a-half-foot-high
metal milk can.

He was serene,
as passersby
strolled or rode their
bicycles.
At first I did not comprehend
how simple it was. To sit
in the shade of the sidewalk trees, painting;
offering lessons
from eleven to noon.

There must be something
more to this
I thought.
But now, I think not.

The can turned slowly
from gray rusty ignominy
to blushful blue dawn enchantment
and the artist made yellow flowers
by daubing them into place
with a bit of ragged cork.

Old man, no older than me no doubt
you will never know
how delighted I was to see you!
painting the old milk can
back to life
in this hidden place
where children grow up watching

or ignoring you paint
and at night play hide-and-seek
in this corner
of our obscure
but extraordinary
village street.

the village of Guadalupe

Taking My Seat

Taking my seat
I bow
to my arrow.

Breathing in
I thank my teachers
who are
all around me.

Breathing out
I thank them
more.